Mr. Beaver and The Paddle

Eighty Acres Publishing

Bobby Brown Bear
Scotty Squirrel
Farmer's Boat House
Daisy Deer
Edward Bald eagle
Rocky Racoon
Duke and Doris duck
Suzy skunk
Pamela Porcupine
Mr. and Mrs. Beaver

Farmer's House
Rusty Red Squirrel
Fisher Brothers Frank &Freddy
Gus the Goose
Jimmy Coyote
Big Benny Bunny
Robby Rabbit

ISBN: 978-1-0691004-0-5

Illustrated by Hooria Batool

www.emilyteichrib.com

Eighty Acres Publishing
Box 194
Gladstone, MB
R0J0T0

Printed in Canada

To the Beaver,
that really did steal my paddle.

In the woods behind a farm
was a stream flowing with
fresh, clean water. There were
many trees and animals.
The Beavers lived in a lodge on
that stream. It was a clear
morning, with blue skies when
Mr. Beaver poked his head out
through the hole on the side of
his lodge.
"Betty dear," said old Mr.
Beaver to his wife, "I am going
out to enjoy this beautiful day."

"I wish you would fix that hole," said Betty Beaver. But Mr. Beaver didn't stay to listen and dove out through the hole in the wall and under the water, instead of using the door. The real entrance to the beaver's lodge was a secret door under the water.

Full of energy, Mr. Beaver swam quickly through the water and popped out next to the riverbank. He climbed out of the river and shook the water off his thick brown fur. The sun was warm, and before long Mr. Beaver found himself wandering down the winding path beside the river. He started to look for a tasty snack, some poplar bark or willows.

He was so focused on his snack that he did not hear the footsteps.

"Hello there Mr. Beaver," came a voice from behind him. Mr. Beaver nearly jumped out of his fur! There stood Robby Rabbit.

"Don't scare a fellow like that," warned Mr. Beaver.

Robby smiled slightly but did not laugh out loud like most of the forest animals would have done. Rabbits were supposed to be happy and hoppy, but not Robby. He always thought things through before he did them. He never laughed at anyone, no matter how funny it looked.

Robby was a young rabbit with fur that was turning from white to brown, for it was the spring of the year. When spring comes all rabbits changed their coats. Mr. Beaver thought that Robby's mixed coat looked very funny. He didn't say anything for he knew that not all the little forest animals had a lovely coat like he did. Mr. Beaver was very proud of the thick watertight coat that he wore.

"What are you doing today, Robby," asked Mr. Beaver warmly, "it's a beautiful day, isn't it?"

"Indeed, it is, but there is something curious." For such a young rabbit, Robby sounded very serious. "The farmer is back on the water with some sort of contraption!! Very curious, yes sir, yes sir." Robby turned to point down the river where he had seen the farmer.

"What kind of contraption?" Mr. Beaver was now himself very interested in this 'curious contraption'.

"It's big, they sit in it, then they hit the water with sticks," Robby told him.

Mr. Beaver frowned, "they hit the water? Are they trying to warn others of danger?" Mr. Beaver was thinking of how he would hit the water with his tail to warn others if he saw danger. That couldn't be it! Maybe the farmer drove it like one of his cars?

"I will have to see it for myself," Mr. Beaver mumbled and with that he left Robby Rabbit sitting on the bank and slid into the water. Mr. Beaver could swim much faster than he could walk, and he was eager to reach the farmer's house further down the river.

After a few minutes of swimming, he was at the edge of the bank looking up at the farmer's house. There, just like Robby had said, was a 'curious contraption' tied to the edge of the bank. Mr. Beaver had never seen anything like it before, but what he saw hooked on to the large contraption was even more interesting. It was like a stick but different. It was long and flat at the end. It reminded Mr. Beaver of his very own tail and Mr. Beaver liked his tail, so he immediately liked this stick!

Mr. Beaver swam over to the strange stick. He smelt it. He felt it. It was a stick all right, but what a funny shape it had grown in! Mr. Beaver had never seen such a thing before. He took the funny looking stick and put it in the water. It floated like a stick. Mr. Beaver tried to pull it under the water, but it didn't sink! So, he crawled up onto the flat part of the stick.

It was a very comfortable spot to be and all at once a bright idea came into his mind. Mr. Beaver had just found the perfect stick to fix the hole in his house. As fast as Mr. Beaver's little legs could kick, he swam home with his new stick.

Mr. Beaver started to fix the crack in his lodge. An hour later he stood back to admire his repair work. Oh, how nice his lodge looked! The next day Mr. and Mrs. Beaver woke up to a terrible racket!

The farmer was standing right next to their house. NO, the farmer was climbing right up onto their lodge! It was terrifying! Mr. and Mrs. Beaver dove out from their lodge through their under-water door and popped up far from their home. They watched in horror as the farmer ripped the new stick out of their lodge making an even bigger hole then before. The farmer had never disturbed them, why would he start now?

The farmer left and the Beavers went to look at their poor lodge, "LOOK AT IT, LOOK AT IT!" Exclaimed Mrs. Beaver, "all that work wasted and for what reason?!!"

Mr. Beaver shook his head, "I don't know."

"Well, I know," Edward Bald Eagle swooped down landing on a branch above them.

"Really!" said Mr. Beaver. He was feeling very cross, "why would the farmer wreck our house?"

Edward Bald Eagle ruffled up his feathers to make himself look bigger and said, "If it doesn't belong to you, you can't have it. You can only lose what is yours to keep."

"What does that mean!?" Mr. Beaver was very upset, "that was my stick and there is only one thing to do, and that is to get my stick back!!"

A little while later Mr. Beaver found his stick sitting beside the contraption and once again brought it back to fix his lodge. The very next day the farmer was back and stole the stick again!

"Maybe," poor Mrs. Beaver quaked, as they watched the farmer wreck their home for the second time. "We should just let the farmer keep the stick; he seems to really like it."

"No," Mr. Beaver said firmly, "that is my stick, I found it fair and square!" So off he went to get his stick back.

Mr. Beaver was back at the farm in no time at all. However, when he got to the contraption, there was no stick. Mr. Beaver slowly made his way to the riverbank and towards the farmer's house, all the while looking for his stick. On the side of the bank, he came to a small open building. He went in and there he spotted it hanging on the wall. Not only one stick, but several different kinds of sticks. Mr. Beaver didn't even have time to wonder why there were so many odd shaped sticks before.....

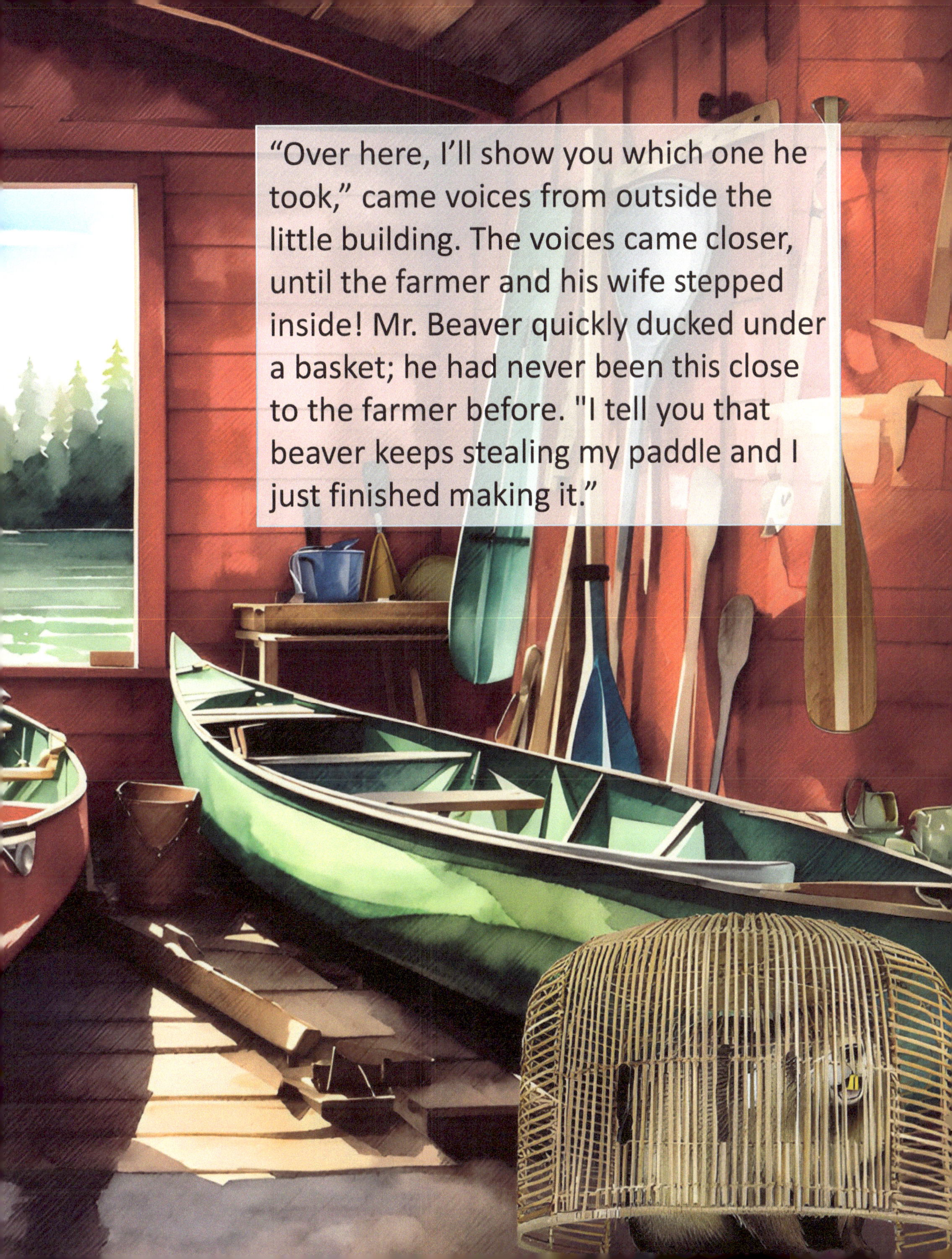

"Over here, I'll show you which one he took," came voices from outside the little building. The voices came closer, until the farmer and his wife stepped inside! Mr. Beaver quickly ducked under a basket; he had never been this close to the farmer before. "I tell you that beaver keeps stealing my paddle and I just finished making it."

Mr. Beaver felt his cheeks start to blush beneath his fur. He knew that stealing was wrong. He thought the farmer had stolen his stick, but it was 'he' who had stolen the farmer's paddle. Now he knew why Edward Bald Eagle said,

"If it doesn't belong to you, you can't have it. You can only lose what is yours to keep."

The paddle was never Mr. Beaver's to keep. When the farmer left Mr. Beaver snuck out of the little building and back down to the river where he headed home to fix the hole in his lodge.

Mr. Beaver swam slowly home; he felt ashamed of what he had done. He knew that he had to fix the hole without the paddle. As Mr. Beaver turned the corner, he got the shock of his life. THERE was the farmer putting a pile of sticks beside his lodge!

"There you go little fella," the farmer said gently. "Now you won't be needing my paddle."

Mr. Beaver felt warmth flow through him. The farmer knew he meant no harm, and Mr. Beaver knew that the farmer had meant no harm to them.

Anyone who has been stealing must steal no longer, but must work, doing something useful with their own hands, that they may have something to share with those in need.

Ephesians 4:28